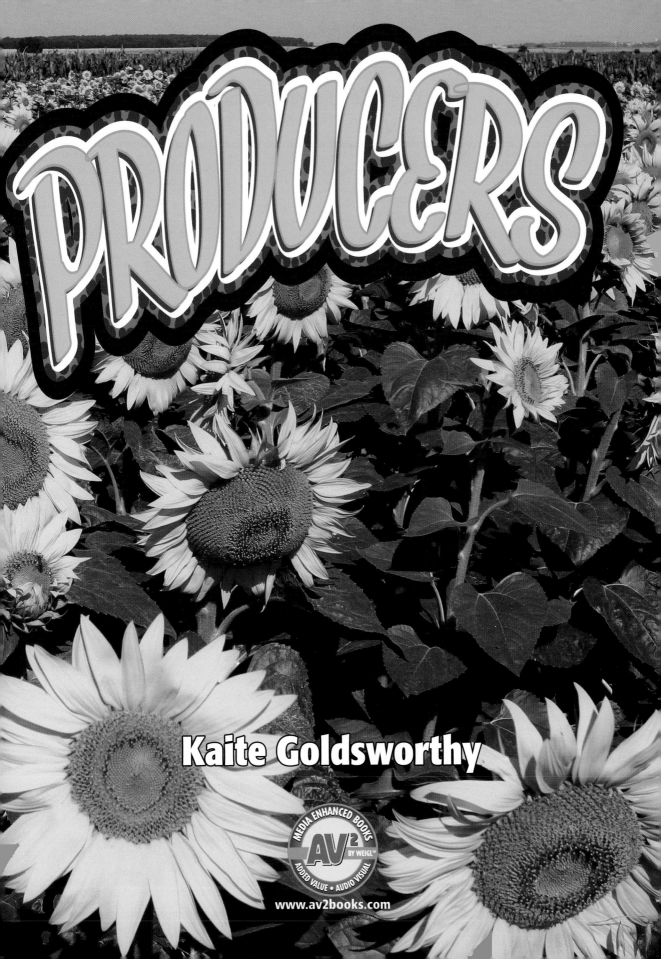

PRODUCERS

Kaite Goldsworthy

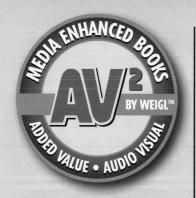

AV² provides enriched content that supplements and complements this book. Weigl's AV² books strive to create inspired learning and engage young minds in a total learning experience.

Your AV² Media Enhanced books come alive with...

Audio
Listen to sections of the book read aloud.

Key Words
Study vocabulary, and complete a matching word activity.

Video
Watch informative video clips.

Quizzes
Test your knowledge.

Embedded Weblinks
Gain additional information for research.

Slide Show
View images and captions, and prepare a presentation.

Try This!
Complete activities and hands-on experiments.

Go to **www.av2books.com**, and enter this book's unique code.

BOOK CODE

D 6 9 0 3 2 3

AV² by Weigl brings you media enhanced books that support active learning.

... and much, much more!

Published by AV² by Weigl
350 5th Avenue, 59th Floor
New York, NY 10118
Website: www.av2books.com   www.weigl.com

Library of Congress Cataloging-in-Publication Data

Goldsworthy, Kaite.
 Producers / Kaite Goldsworthy.
    p. cm. — (Food chains)
 Includes index.
 ISBN 978-1-61690-710-5 (hardcover: alk. paper) — ISBN 978-1-61690-716-7 (softcover: alk. paper)
 1. Photosynthesis—Juvenile literature. 2. Plants—Juvenile literature. I. Title.
 QK882.G65 2011
 581.7'16—dc22   2010051001

Printed in the United States of America in North Mankato, Minnesota
1 2 3 4 5 6 7 8 9 0 15 14 13 12 11

062011
WEP290411

Project Coordinator Aaron Carr
Art Director Terry Paulhus

Photo Credits
Every reasonable effort has been made to trace ownership and to obtain permission to reprint copyright material. The publishers would be pleased to have any errors or omissions brought to their attention so that they may be corrected in subsequent printings.

Weigl acknowledges Getty Images as its primary image supplier for this title.

Contents

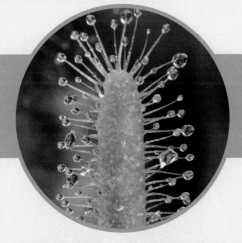

Nature's Food Chain

All living things need food to survive. Food provides the **energy** that plants and animals need to grow and thrive.

Plants and animals do not rely on the same types of food to live. Plants make their own food. They use energy from the Sun and water from the soil. Some animals eat plants. Others eat animals that have already eaten plants. In this way, all living things are connected to each other. These connections form food chains.

A food chain is made up of **producers** and **consumers**. Plants are the main producers in a food chain. This is because they make energy. This energy can be used by the rest of the living things on Earth. The other living things are called consumers.

There are five types of consumers in a food chain. They are carnivores, decomposers, herbivores, omnivores, and parasites. All of the world's organisms belong to one of these groups in the food chain.

Certain trees grow in the shape of a triangle so more of their lower branches reach the Sun.

Soaking Up Sunlight

Plants and their parts are shaped in ways that help them take in sunlight.

FOOD CHAIN

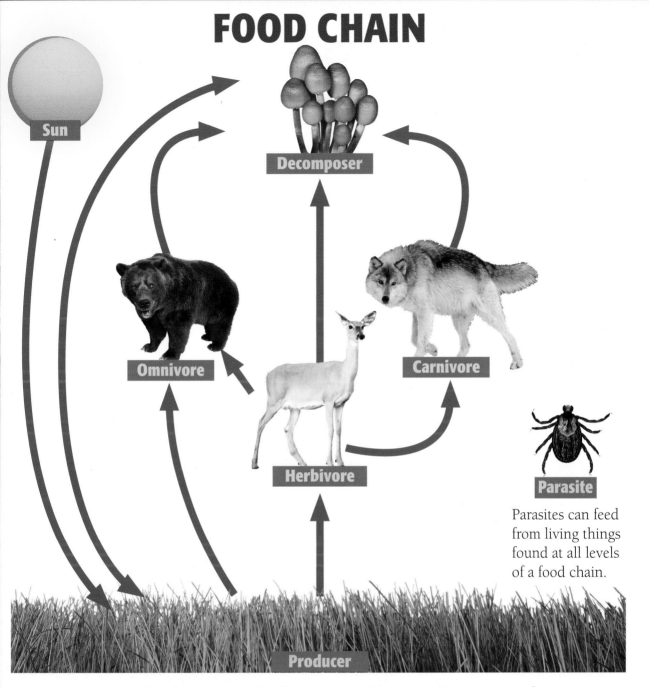

In this example, the Sun starts the food chain by providing energy for grass to grow. The deer eats grass as its food, and the wolf eats the deer. Bears may also eat grass or deer. Mushrooms receive energy from grass and the waste left behind by wolves, deer, and bears. Parasites can be found at any point along the food chain. They can live inside or on producers and consumers. A tick can get the food it needs to survive from a deer, a bear, or a wolf.

What Is a Producer?

All of the green plants on Earth are producers. They are a kind of producer called an **autotroph**. This means they are able to produce their own food through a process called photosynthesis. In this process, plants use sunlight and other materials, such as water and **minerals**, to make sugar and oxygen. Plants use the sugar they produce for the energy they need to grow. The oxygen plants produce is put into the air.

Animals breathe in the oxygen that plants produce. Many animals also consume plants as a source of food. An animal that eats a plant uses the plant's sugar and other materials for energy. Without producers, no other forms of life would be possible.

There are about 30,000 types of plants that humans can eat. Some are well known, such as blueberries. Others, such as daylily flowers, are less commonly eaten.

Producers are part of every food chain. Each **ecosystem** has a different food chain. The food chain in a city park is not the same as the one found in a lake. The producers in a park include plants such as grass. A lake has underwater plants.

A lake also has producers called algae and bacteria. Algae are like plants in some ways. Most algae produce their own food using sunlight. However, algae do not **reproduce** the way plants do. Bacteria are living things that are one **cell** in size. Bacteria are found everywhere. Some types are autotrophs. Both algae and bacteria are eaten by consumers such as snails.

A farm is an ecosystem that people control. Producers are found on farms and in other ecosystems.

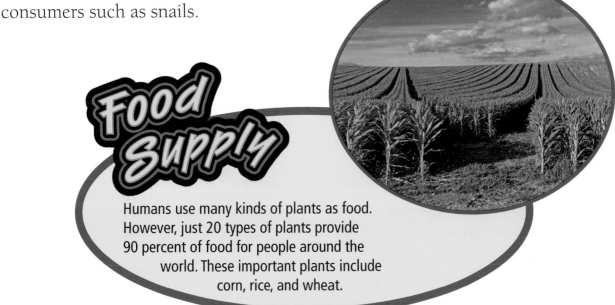

Food Supply

Humans use many kinds of plants as food. However, just 20 types of plants provide 90 percent of food for people around the world. These important plants include corn, rice, and wheat.

Built for Producing

Imagine being able to make food in your own body. That is what plants, algae, and some bacteria do through photosynthesis. The word *photosynthesis* comes from two Greek words. They are *photo*, which means "light," and *synthesis*, which means "putting together."

There are four conditions needed for plant photosynthesis. First, plants need energy to produce food. They receive this energy from the Sun. Next, plants need water. They absorb water mainly through their roots. Plants also need carbon dioxide. That is one of the gases that make up air. Finally, plants use **chlorophyll**, which is found in plant cells. Chlorophyll is green, which is why the leaves of most plants are green.

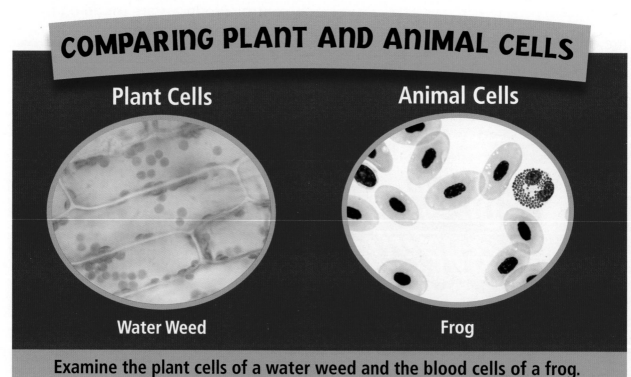

COMPARING PLANT AND ANIMAL CELLS

Plant Cells

Water Weed

Animal Cells

Frog

Examine the plant cells of a water weed and the blood cells of a frog. What differences do you see?

Think of the plant as a food factory. Chlorophyll in the leaves takes in energy from the Sun. The roots take in water. Water is made of hydrogen and oxygen. The plant uses the Sun's energy to break water into its parts. The leaves also take in carbon dioxide. The hydrogen then joins with the carbon dioxide to make food called carbohydrates, or sugar. The food spreads through the plant. The leftover oxygen is released through tiny holes on the leaf, called **stomata**. Most of the process takes place in less than one second.

The largest known organism is a stand of aspen trees in Utah. The trees appear to be separate but are one living being. They share one network of roots.

Recycled Air

Producers take in carbon dioxide and release oxygen into the air. Humans breathe in the oxygen and breathe out carbon dioxide. Plants and people help one another.

Producers in Practice

Plants come in many sizes, from tiny clover to tall oak trees. Most plants begin life as a tiny seed. The seed needs three things to **germinate**. Heat, water, and soil are needed to start the seed's growth. The seed sends roots down into the soil. It sends **shoots** upward toward the Sun.

When the first leaves emerge, the plant is a seedling. Then, the plant is ready to produce its own food. Each seed has the **nutrients** a new plant needs until leaves appear and the plant is ready to make its own food.

Not long ago, a 2,000-year-old date palm seed was planted successfully. Some seeds can go many years before sprouting. This allows the seeds to wait for good growing conditions.

Most plants have similar parts. They have leaves or needles. These parts are very important, because photosynthesis occurs in them. A plant's roots take in water and minerals from the soil. The roots also help hold the plant in place in the ground. The stem carries the water and minerals from the roots. The stem also carries the sugar produced by the leaves or needles to the rest of the plant. Stems can be woody, such as a tree trunk. They can also be soft, such as a flower's stem.

Most plants also have parts that help them reproduce from seeds. In many plants, these parts are in the flowers. In plants such as strawberries, the flowers become fruit, which holds the plant's seeds. In plants such as pine trees, the seeds are found in cones. Plants such as mosses, however, are made of cells that can split in two. Mosses and similar plants reproduce in this manner.

On many plants, fruit holds the seeds. An animal eats the fruit. The seeds pass through the animal's body. The seeds then drop to the ground in the animal's waste.

Spreading Seeds

Animals spread seeds around in their waste. They can also carry seeds in their mouths or on their feathers or fur, then drop them somewhere else. Seeds are carried by wind and water, too. Some plants even have the ability to shoot their seeds, in order to spread the seeds farther.

Meat-eating Plants

The Venus's-flytrap is a producer. It uses photosynthesis as the main source of its nutrients. However, the Venus's-flytrap is also a consumer. It is an example of a carnivore, which means it eats meat. The plant traps and digests insects and tiny animals such as spiders. The Venus's-flytrap eats meat as a way to take in minerals.

The trap of a Venus's-flytrap can capture insects just four or five times. After that, the trap dies. If there are enough nutrients, a bigger trap grows.

There are more than 450 **species** of carnivorous plants in the world. Plants of the same species share certain characteristics. These characteristics can include how the leaves are shaped or how the petals look.

Most carnivorous plants are found in swamps and bogs. These places do not support many kinds of plants. The right nutrients are not available. However, carnivorous plants have **adapted** by adding insects to their diets. Some of the most common carnivorous plants include pitcher plants and sundews.

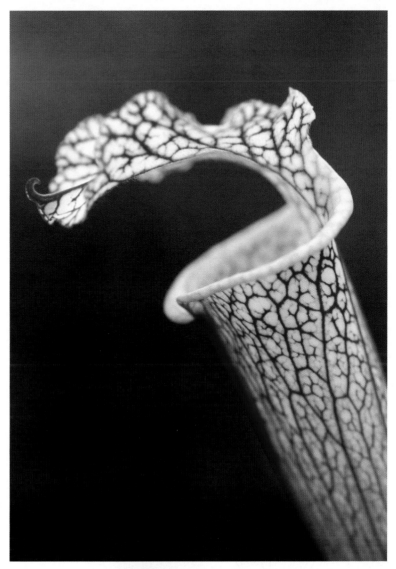

Many carnivorous plants produce a sweet-smelling odor to attract insects. When insects come near, they become trapped in the plant's leaves. The leaves release juices that help break down the insect.

Some kinds of pitcher plants are about the size of a person's fist. Other kinds can be as much as 3 feet (1 meter) tall.

Producer Close-ups

There are many kinds of producers. They come in all shapes and sizes. Some producers are very large, while others are tiny.

Bull Kelp

+ largest type of brown algae
+ found along the coast of the northeast Pacific Ocean
+ grows by as much as 2 feet (0.6 meters) in a single day and can be 200 feet (61 meters) long
+ the wide base, or "holdfast," anchors the plant to rocks or the ocean floor
+ made up of a round, hollow bulb, which traps air like a balloon, allowing it to float and absorb sunlight
+ provides both food and nesting areas for marine creatures such as birds, seals, and sea otters

Saguaro Cactus

+ largest cactus in the United States
+ found only in the Sonoran Desert of the southwestern United States
+ can live from 150 to 200 years
+ can grow as tall as 40 to 60 feet (12 to 18 meters)
+ can have as many as 25 upward "arms" over time
+ its red fruit is eaten by animals such as cactus wrens, jackrabbits, and coyotes

Elephant Grass

+ grows by lakes and rivers on African grasslands
+ can grow as tall as 10 to 14 feet (3 to 4 meters)
+ has yellow or purple hairy stems
+ leaves have very sharp edges
+ uses its root system to reproduce
+ many birds nest in the grass, and animals such as elephants and zebras eat the grass

Purple Saxifrage

+ common in Arctic regions, Greenland, the Alps, and the Rocky Mountains
+ plant grows best in cold climates
+ found low to the ground in clumps
+ produces small purple or lilac flowers that can be eaten
+ flowers appear when the snow melts.
+ source of food for the Arctic hare and other cold-climate animals

White Birch

+ **deciduous** tree found in colder climates of North America
+ also known as "paper birch" because the white, papery bark peels easily
+ can live up to 140 years
+ can grow as high as 80 feet (24 meters)
+ moose, deer, porcupines, rabbits, squirrels, and other forest animals feed on the leaves, bark, and shoots

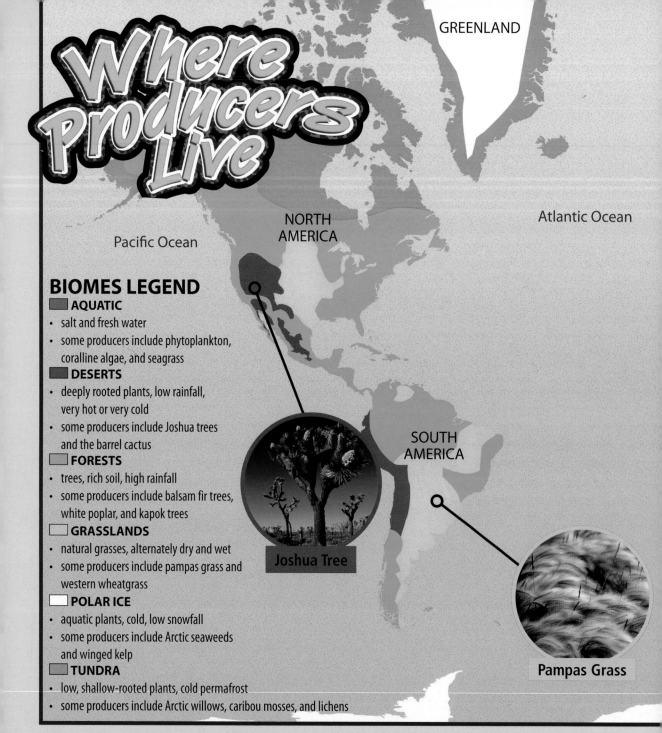

Where Producers Live

GREENLAND

Atlantic Ocean

NORTH AMERICA

Pacific Ocean

BIOMES LEGEND

AQUATIC
- salt and fresh water
- some producers include phytoplankton, coralline algae, and seagrass

DESERTS
- deeply rooted plants, low rainfall, very hot or very cold
- some producers include Joshua trees and the barrel cactus

FORESTS
- trees, rich soil, high rainfall
- some producers include balsam fir trees, white poplar, and kapok trees

GRASSLANDS
- natural grasses, alternately dry and wet
- some producers include pampas grass and western wheatgrass

POLAR ICE
- aquatic plants, cold, low snowfall
- some producers include Arctic seaweeds and winged kelp

TUNDRA
- low, shallow-rooted plants, cold permafrost
- some producers include Arctic willows, caribou mosses, and lichens

SOUTH AMERICA

Joshua Tree

Pampas Grass

All producers require special living conditions in order to thrive. The place where a producer lives is called its habitat. Earth has many different **biomes** that serve as habitats. Biomes are defined by their climates and by the plants and animals that live there. The world's largest biomes are aquatic, deserts, forests, grasslands, polar ice, and tundra.

A producer's habitat can be as big as a desert or a forest. It can also be as small as a pond. Each producer must live where it can get the sunlight and water it needs to survive. For example, aquatic producers usually live near the water's

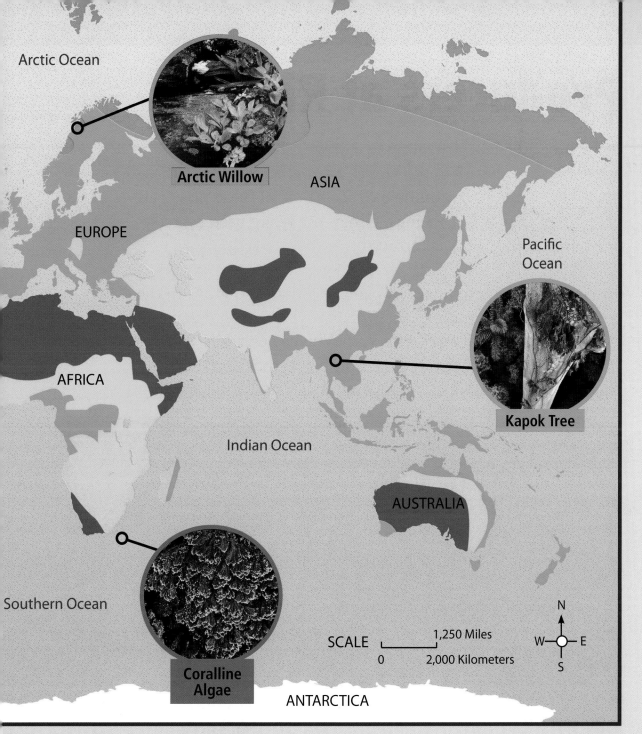

Arctic Ocean

Arctic Willow

ASIA

EUROPE

Pacific Ocean

Kapok Tree

AFRICA

Indian Ocean

AUSTRALIA

Southern Ocean

Coralline Algae

ANTARCTICA

SCALE

1,250 Miles

0   2,000 Kilometers

N
W — E
S

surface in order to receive sunlight for photosynthesis.

A producer that lives in a biome in one part of the world might not live in the same biome in a different part of the world. For example, the grasses found in Africa's grasslands are different from those in North American grasslands.

Look at the map to see where some types of producers may live. Can you think of other producers? Where on the map do they live?

Producers at Risk

Some producers are struggling to survive. There are about 400,000 plant species in the world. More than 80,000 of these plants are at risk of becoming **extinct**. Some of these plants are being used to make medicines. Others are being used to make items for people, such as furniture.

The list of Earth's **endangered** plants continues to grow. In the United States, for example, the Arizona cypress is in danger of dying out, as is the fishhook cactus. When a species is at risk, it is often a sign that there are larger problems that need correction. Changes in water, soil, and temperature affect how plants grow.

Every year, between 3 billion and 6 billion trees are cut down.

Most scientists believe that Earth's climate has been getting warmer in recent years. This change is known as global warming. The rise in temperature affects plants on land. It also changes life for plants in the ocean. Warmer temperatures make it more difficult for some plants to live and reproduce. Some plants are hardy and can adapt to the new conditions. Others cannot. In some places, the plants dry out, which makes it easier for fires to start. Many plants are facing challenges.

BOTANIST

Career
A botanist is a scientist who specializes in the study of plants. There are many different fields within botany to study.

Education
A minimum of a bachelor's degree in biology or a related science is needed. Many jobs require a master's or doctorate degree. Speaking another language can be useful for the study of plants in other countries.

Working Conditions
Working environments range from classrooms and laboratories to outdoor field locations. Botanist work around the globe in all biomes.

Tools
Field Equipment: magnifying glass, compass, pencil, sketchbook, trowel, pruner, bags for specimen collection, camera, plant press, field guide, maps

Lab Equipment: microscope, slides, dissecting needle, ruler, labels

Doing Our Part

Ebony trees are prized for their dark wood. There are hundreds of species. Most are now endangered. Special programs protect rare, endangered plants, such as ebony trees. In addition, the habitats of many endangered producers are protected by law. Protecting these plants also helps the animals in their food chains.

Making an Energy Pyramid

A food chain is one way to chart the transfer of energy from one living thing to another. Another way to show how living things are connected is through an energy pyramid. An energy pyramid starts with the Sun. The Sun provides the source of energy that allows producers to grow. Producers are a source of energy for primary consumers in the next level of the pyramid. Primary consumers transfer energy up the pyramid to tertiary consumers. In this way, all living things depend on one another for survival. In the example below, grass provides food for rabbits, and rabbits are food for wolves.

ENERGY PYRAMID

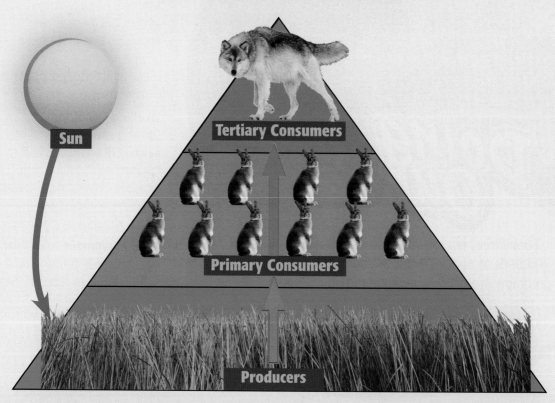

Below are some examples of producers and the habitats where they live. Choose one of the producers and learn more about it. Using the Internet and your school library, find information about the producer. Determine which animals rely on the producer for food. Using your producer as the base, draw an energy pyramid showing the transfer of energy. Which primary consumers feed on the plant or the kind of algae that you picked? Which tertiary consumers receive energy from the primary consumers in your energy pyramid?

PRODUCERS

AQUATIC	Brown Algae	Kelp	Pond Lilies
DESERTS	Prickly Pear Cactus	Ocotillo	Date Palm
FORESTS	Oak Tree	Durian	Lady Fern
GRASSLANDS	Senegal Gum Acacia	Bermuda Grass	Buffalo Grass
TUNDRA	Arctic Moss	Bearberry	Arctic Liverwort

Quick Quiz

Based on what you have just read, try to answer the following questions correctly.

1. **What is an autotroph?**

2. **What type of biome would phytoplankton be found in?**

3. **What gas do producers give off during photosynthesis?**

4. **Approximately how many species of plants are there in the world?**

5. **How long does the process of photosynthesis take?**

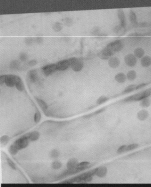

6. **How do consumers help producers reproduce?**

7. **What is chlorophyll?**

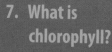

8. **What four components are required for photosynthesis to take place?**

Answers: 1. An organism that can produce its own food **2.** The ocean **3.** Oxygen **4.** 400,000 **5.** Less than a second **6.** By consuming fruit and then spreading the seeds **7.** Chlorophyll is the green pigment found in the leaves of plants. It is needed for photosynthesis. **8.** Energy from the sun, water, carbon dioxide, chlorophyll

Glossary

adapted: changed over time to fit an environment

autotroph: an organism that is able to make its own food

biomes: large areas with the same climate and other natural conditions in which certain kinds of plants and animals live

cell: the smallest unit that all living things are made of

chlorophyll: a substance in green plants needed for photosynthesis

consumers: animals that feed on plants or other animals

deciduous: sheds leaves each year

ecosystem: a community of living things and the environment where they live

endangered: at risk of no longer living any place on Earth

energy: the usable power living things receive from food that they use to grow and stay healthy

extinct: no longer living any place on Earth

germinate: to begin growth or development

minerals: substances that occur in nature and that many living things need in small amounts

nutrients: substances that provide food for plants and animals

producers: living things, such as plants, that produce their own food

reproduce: to produce new individuals of the same kind

shoots: stems or branches that are not yet fully grown

species: a group of the same kind of living things; members can breed together

stomata: tiny openings on a plant part such as a leaf, through which oxygen and other gases go in and out

Index

Log on to www.av2books.com

AV² by Weigl brings you media enhanced books that support active learning. Go to www.av2books.com, and enter the special code found on page 2 of this book. You will gain access to enriched and enhanced content that supplements and complements this book. Content includes video, audio, web links, quizzes, a slide show, and activities.

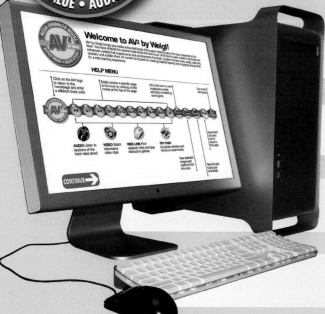

Audio
Listen to sections of the book read aloud.

Video
Watch informative video clips.

Embedded Weblinks
Gain additional information for research.

Try This!
Complete activities and hands-on experiments.

WHAT'S ONLINE?

Try This!	**Embedded Weblinks**	**Video**	**EXTRA FEATURES**
Test your knowledge of food chains.	Discover more producers.	Watch a video introduction to producers.	**Audio** Listen to sections of the book read aloud.
Outline the features of a producer.	Learn more about one of the producers in this book.	Watch a video about a producer.	
Research a producer.	Find out more about producer conservation efforts.		**Key Words** Study vocabulary, and complete a matching word activity.
Compare producers that live in different areas.	Learn more about producers.		
Try an interactive activity.			**Slide Show** View images and captions, and prepare a presentation.
			Quizzes Test your knowledge.

AV² was built to bridge the gap between print and digital. We encourage you to tell us what you like and what you want to see in the future.
Sign up to be an AV² Ambassador at www.av2books.com/ambassador.